DARING AND DANGEROUS

AUTO RACERS

ANASTASIA SUEN

Rourke
Educational Media
rourkeeducationalmedia.com

Before, During, and After Reading Activities

Before Reading: Building Background Knowledge and Academic Vocabulary

"Before Reading" strategies activate prior knowledge and set a purpose for reading. Before reading a book, it is important to tap into what your child or students already know about the topic. This will help them develop their vocabulary and increase their reading comprehension.

Questions and activities to build background knowledge:
1. Look at the cover of the book. What will this book be about?
2. What do you already know about the topic?
3. Let's study the Table of Contents. What will you learn about in the book's chapters?
4. What would you like to learn about this topic? Do you think you might learn about it from this book? Why or why not?

Building Academic Vocabulary
Building academic vocabulary is critical to understanding subject content.
Assist your child or students to gain meaning of the following vocabulary words.
Content Area Vocabulary
Read the list. What do these words mean?
- accelerator
- debris
- intact
- slide job
- spectators
- sponsor

During Reading: Writing Component

"During Reading" strategies help to make connections, monitor understanding, generate questions, and stay focused.
1. While reading, write in your reading journal any questions you have or anything you do not understand.
2. After completing each chapter, write a summary of the chapter in your reading journal.
3. While reading, make connections with the text and write them in your reading journal.
   a) Text to Self – What does this remind me of in my life? What were my feelings when I read this?
   b) Text to Text – What does this remind me of in another book I've read? How is this different from other books I've read?
   c) Text to World – What does this remind me of in the real world? Have I heard about this before? (News, current events, school, etc....)

After Reading: Comprehension and Extension Activity

"After Reading" strategies provide an opportunity to summarize, question, reflect, discuss, and respond to text. After reading the book, work on the following questions with your child or students to check their level of reading comprehension and content mastery.
1. Why is auto racing dangerous? (Summarize)
2. Why do sponsors want their names on the cars and the fire suits? (Infer)
3. Who wears a helmet and a fire suit? (Asking Questions)
4. Where is the safest place for you to sit and watch an auto race? (Text to Self)

Extension Activity
Find out more about professional auto racing. Research a race track near you. How big is the track? What kind of races does it sponsor? Who has won races at this track? Did these drivers begin their careers by racing karts?

TABLE OF CONTENTS

THE RACE BEFORE THE RACE

Drivers have to qualify for every race. This determines how the cars line up. The fastest car gets the pole position. A **sponsor** likes to see their name at the front of the line.

 sponsor (SPON-sur): a person or a group that gives money to pay for an advertisement

Alex Bowman and crew

Robert Hight broke his own **record** twice! First, he broke a record by driving 337.66 miles (543.41 kilometers) per hour.

Two months later, he drove his Funny Car at 339.87 miles (546.97 kilometers) per hour!

 record (REK-urd): something faster, bigger, or better than anyone has ever done it before

MECHANICAL
FAILURE

The parade laps began. The cars drove slowly around the track. Then Conor Daly's car caught fire. The side of his car said, "Fueled by Bacon."

Before the Indianapolis 500, the racers follow the pace car around the track to warm up.

WIPER

DISPLAY

DRINK

A Racing Family

Adam Petty was a fourth-generation NASCAR driver. His great-grandfather Lee was one of the first NASCAR drivers. His grandfather Richard was called "The King." His father Kyle won his first race at age 19.

The **accelerator** in Adam Petty's car got stuck during practice. The car crashed into the wall. After Adam's death, NASCAR added a red button to the steering wheel. It turns off the car.

 accelerator (ak-SEL-uhr-ayt-uhr): a device for controlling the speed of a motor vehicle engine

CRASHES AND COLLISIONS

In a race's first lap, Simon Pagenaud headed for turn one. His car was hit from behind. The car was damaged before it reached full speed. Simon was out of the race.

Kevin Ward Jr. spun out after Tony Stewart made a **slide job** move. After his car spun out, Kevin ran across the track. The back of Tony's car hit Kevin. Kevin died later that night.

☢ **slide job** (SLIDE job): a dirt track move where one car passes another car by sliding into a turn so it lands in front of the other car

Kevin was driving a winged sprint car like this one.

In 1955, there were only a few bales of hay between the grandstands and the Le Mans race track. A crash on the track ended up in the crowd. Many people died.

When drivers waited on their marks to begin the 24 Hours of Le Mans race in 1960, there were two walls in front of the grandstands.

The Dakar Rally is a 14-day race. It does not take place on an official race track. In 2016, a car drove into the crowd. Eleven **spectators** were injured.

☢ **spectators** (SPEK-tay-turs): people who watch an event

The Dakar Rally

A French racer got lost in the African desert in 1977. The next year, he decided to race from his home in Paris to Dakar, Senegal. The Dakar Rally moved to South America in 2009.

Pit crew work can be dangerous too. The pit crew moves around the car as they work. If anyone is near the car when it moves, they can get hurt.

Accidents can happen anytime. Cars bump into each other. They spin out of control. Dale Earnhardt Sr. crashed in the last lap of the 2001 Daytona 500. He was killed instantly.

Driver Safety

After the 2001 accident, NASCAR made changes to protect the drivers. Every car had to have a HANS device. HANS stands for Head And Neck Safety.

The last race of the IndyCar season was cancelled after a crash in 2011. Fifteen of the 34 cars on the track crashed in Lap 11.

Collisions damage cars. They are dangerous for drivers. During a crash, **debris** flies all over the track.

debris (duh-BREE): the pieces that are left after something breaks

Collisions happen often during a race. If the car is still **intact**, the driver can finish the race.

⚛ **intact** (in-TAKT): not broken

MEMORY GAME

Can you match the image to what you read?

INDEX

SHOW WHAT YOU KNOW

1. Why do drivers have to qualify for the race?

2. What happened to Kevin Ward Jr.?

3. Why did NASCAR add a red button to the steering wheel?

4. Namc three ways cars can race.

5. What can happen when one car loses control during a race?

FURTHER READING

Niver, Heather Moore, *Racing's Greatest Records*, Powerkids Press, 2015.

Savage, Jeff, *Auto Racing Super Stats*, Lerner Publishing Group, 2017.

Weber, M., *Wild Moments of Sports Car Racing*, Capstone Press, 2018.

ABOUT THE AUTHOR

Anastasia Suen is the author of more than 300 books for young readers, including *Go-Kart Rush* (written with the pen name Jake Maddox). She reads, writes, and edits books in her studio in Northern California.

Meet The Author!
www.meetREMauthors.com

www.rourkeeducationalmedia.com

PHOTO CREDITS: Cover: ©Hodag Media/ shutterstock.com; page 5: ©Harold Hinson / HHP for Chevy Racing; page 6-7: ©Richard H Shute / Gary Nastase and General Motors; page 8-9: ©Honda; page 10: ©Eric Hameister; page 13, 25, 26, 29: ©Actions Sports Photography; page 15: ©John J Klaiber Jr; page 16: ©Chevy; page 18: cristiano barni; page 21: ©Abdul Razak Latif; page 22: ©HHP / Harold Hinson and General Motors

Edited by: Keli Sipperley
Cover and Interior design by: Rhea Magaro-Wallace

Library of Congress PCN Data

Auto Racers / Anastasia Suen
 (Daring and Dangerous)
  ISBN 978-1-64369-067-4 (hardcover)
  ISBN 978-1-64369-072-8 (soft cover)
  ISBN 978-1-64369-213-5 (e-Book)
Library of Congress Control Number: 2018955847

Rourke Educational Media
Printed in the United States of America,
North Mankato, Minnesota